Facts About Sex

for Today's Youth

SOL GORDON

Illustrated by Vivien Cohen

ED-U PRESS

New Edition, 1979

Copyright © 1969, 1970, 1973, 1978, 1979, by Sol Gordon

New illustrations copyright © 1979 by Vivien Cohen

Library of Congress Cataloging in Publication Data

Gordon, Sol, 1923—
 Facts about sex for today's youth.

 SUMMARY: A simple discussion of various aspects of
sexual maturation including definitions of vulgar or
slang terms in reference to sex and sexual organs.
 First ed. published in 1969 under title: Facts
about sex for exceptional youth. Later ed. published
in 1970 under title: Facts about sex; a basic guide.
 Includes bibliographical references.
 1. Sex education for youth. [1. Sex education
for youth] 1. Cohen, Vivien, illus. II. Title.
HQ35.G65   1973   612.6'007   72-12088
ISBN 0-934978-01-8 (formerly ISBN 0-381-996476)

Manufactured in the United States of America

Contents

The Author

Sol Gordon is a clinical psychologist. He has taught courses in child and adolescent psychology at the University of Pennsylvania, Rutgers University and Yeshiva University. Dr. Gordon is the author of the introductory text *Psychology For You,* and has had many articles published in professional journals. He is currently Professor of Child and Family Studies at Syracuse University, New York.

The Illustrator

Vivien Cohen obtained her B.A. from Pratt Institute, School of Fine and Applied Arts. She has had extensive training and experience as a medical artist. She resides in Woodbridge, New Jersey.

Foreword

The answer to the question: "What should we teach our children about sex?" is to **just teach the facts**. Young people will benefit from facts presented by sensitive and sensible teachers.

Within this concise book, written for adolescents, Sol Gordon presents the **facts** about sex and sexuality. He thereby develops a starting point for meaningful communication about the important role of values as they relate to sex, sexuality and family life.

Reading and understanding this book is a must for every parent of teenagers. Parents of younger children should also read it to be "askable" in future years.

U.G. Turner III, M.D., FACOG
Obstetrician and Gynecologist
Certified Sex Therapist
Charlottesville, Virginia

Author's Introduction

Parents are not always clear on how much their children know—or should know—about sex. Most parents have a tough time when they discuss topics like sexual intercourse and masturbation. As a result, most young people learn about sex from their friends, through the medium of curse words, dirty jokes, graffiti and the distorted and exaggerated views of sex conveyed by television, movies and newspapers.

Many parents feel that knowing "too much" too early leads to sexual misbehavior, but most experts have the opposite view. Children are much more likely to have sexual difficulties if they don't know what sex is all about. Even pornography is not necessarily harmful. Young people who are well informed about sex usually find pornography boring or repulsive.

It is very important for young people to understand sex and to know the language associated with it, including "street" expressions which we have used in a few instances to explain the meaning of difficult words. If teenagers remain uninformed, they tend to be insecure, and are more susceptible to irresponsible behavior.

Adolescents are particularly preoccupied with thoughts about sex because they are experiencing physical and emotional changes. While some behavior can be abnormal, all thoughts, fantasies, dreams and ideas—even if they are about sexual exploits—are normal. People sometimes have thoughts, impulses or dreams which worry them. The more they worry about them, the more often the thoughts recur. It is important to understand that this happens because of guilt feelings. If they knew that all of us have sexual thoughts and desires, they would be less concerned about their own.

Children may want to discuss some of their sexual concerns with their parents. Parents should be able to accept such confidences without making their children feel guilty.

Those of you who have teenage children should read this entire book. Parents of younger children should also read it to prepare themselves for the questions their children will someday ask. If you're not ready with answers, they will ask elsewhere. Although written for adolescents, some ten and eleven-year-olds can profit from this book. The worst that could happen to young children who read it is that they might not understand everything.

Do not be deceived when your child says he or she is not interested in learning about sex. Few boys are willing to admit to adults that they do not know all there is to know about sex, and few girls are willing to admit

2

that they are even interested in sex. If you feel your child is not ready to acknowledge this interest, just leave the book around so he or she can read it privately.

This book is purposely brief because the average young person to whom it is addressed will not read, or may get confused by, a long, detailed or "moralistic" presentation. Most books about sex are written to please uptight parents. It is little wonder that despite the availability of hundreds of sex education books, they are read by relatively few young people.

We hope you will find *Facts About Sex* a starting point for meaningful communication about the larger and **more important** role of values as it relates to sex and family living. This book does make some judgments and includes some controversial issues. We hope that parents will feel free to discuss their own views in a manner that will help their children appreciate the fact that differences of opinion exist in every vital area of human interaction.

In this new edition, it is essential to note the findings of recent research which show that many (if not most) teenagers will have sex before marriage without parental knowledge or consent. We are merely acknowledging the trend; we do not advocate this behavior. As a matter of fact, this book outlines good reasons why teenagers should *not* engage in sexual intercourse. However, in view of the existing facts, we must consider the question—is it not better to use birth control than to bring an unwanted child into this world? Remember too, youths need models, not critics.

This is a sexually developed young woman.

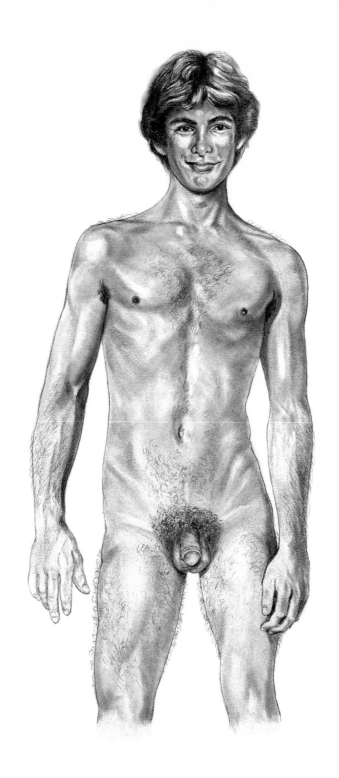

This is a sexually developed young man.

Sex—
In Plain Language

You will read and hear a lot about sex. People talk about it and many television programs emphasize sex in some way. Sex is both emotional and physical. Some people think that the physical part of sex is dirty. They are wrong. Most people, however, feel that sexual acts should be conducted in private by consenting adults. This is what we think too.

When people talk about sex appeal, they usually mean being attractive to the opposite sex. When they talk about "sleeping together," "getting laid," "having sex," "having relations," they usually mean sexual intercourse. Another word for sexual intercourse is coitus. There are several "vulgar" words for sexual intercourse. Ordinary words like "ball," "jump," "making it" and "screw" are also used as impolite ways of referring to sexual intercourse.

Sexual
Intercourse

Sexual intercourse occurs when a man puts his enlarged (erect) penis into the vagina* of a

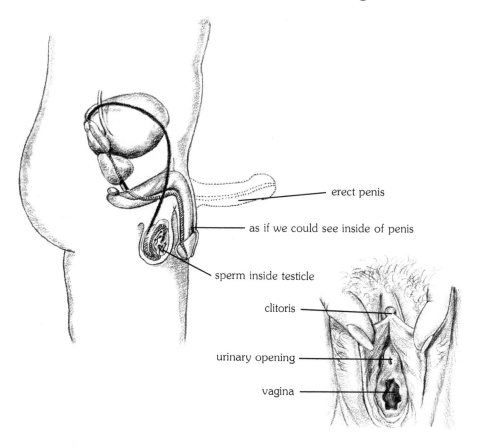

erect penis

as if we could see inside of penis

sperm inside testicle

clitoris

urinary opening

vagina

*Some "street" words for vagina are "box," "snatch," "cunt," "hole," "pussy." It is not polite to use any of these expressions.

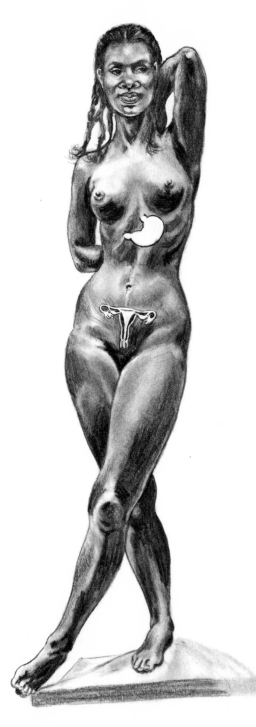

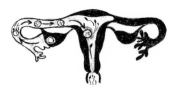

This is the way the sperm from the male (shown greatly enlarged) travels within the woman's body to reach the egg after intercourse takes place.

This is the way the fertilized egg cell grows to become a baby.

woman. Boys sometimes wonder about the chance of urine accidentally coming through the penis while intercourse is taking place. Nature takes care of that. Urine cannot come out during intercourse. The release of the sperm into the vagina is called ejaculation (e-jack-u-lay-shun). After the man ejaculates (comes), the penis loses its erection. It takes a while before the penis can become erect again.

One position for sexual intercourse is when the woman lies on her back and the man lies on top, facing her. However, couples who feel like it vary their positions during sexual relations. Sometimes one partner is more active than the other. No particular position, if it is voluntary and enjoyable, is considered "better" or more "normal" than another.

Before, during and after sexual intercourse, a couple will usually kiss, embrace and stroke each other to show their affection.

Human Reproduction

Human reproduction refers to the creation of a new human being. Most living things, including animals

This is what an unborn fetus looks like as it develops inside the mother's uterus. This picture is shown as though you could see inside the mother's body.

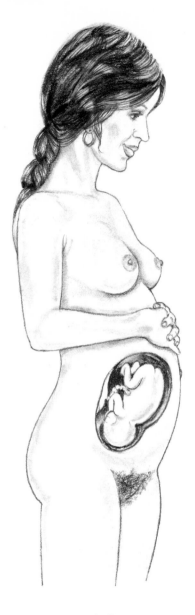

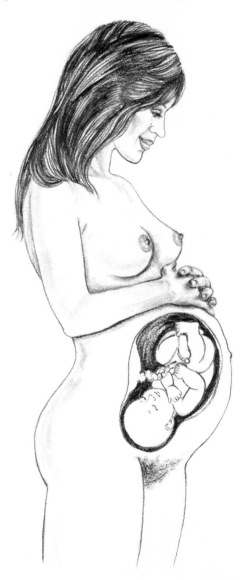

About halfway
through pregnancy

Just before
the baby is born

and plants, need a male and female to reproduce. Human beings can reproduce after they reach puberty. Puberty is the time when a boy is able to make a girl pregnant and the girl is able to have children. After the female reaches puberty, at a certain time of each month, she produces within her body a tiny egg cell called the ovum. After sexual intercourse, if a sperm unites with the egg cell, it is called fertilization. If the fertilized cell attaches to the wall of the uterus, the woman becomes pregnant. This means a fetus is being developed. The place inside the female where it develops is called the uterus. * Womb is another name for the uterus. The baby is called an embryo in the first three months of pregnancy, and a fetus in the remaining months. A full term pregnancy usually last nine months. Sometimes a fetus is expelled from the uterus before it has fully developed. This is called a miscarriage.

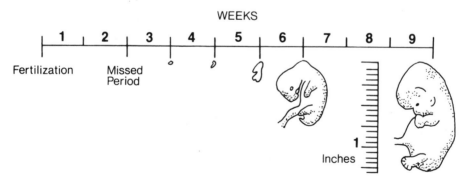

The growth of the embryo (actual sizes). All but a small percentage of miscarriages and abortions occur during the first nine weeks of pregnancy.

*Although people will often speak of the fetus developing in the woman's stomach, this is not correct. The fetus remains in the uterus until birth.

This is the way
a baby is usually born.

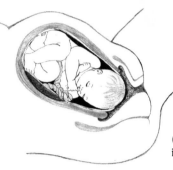

(Shown as if you could see
inside the mother's body.)

The top of the head
begins to show outside.

The head shows
as far as the chin.

A baby is almost born.

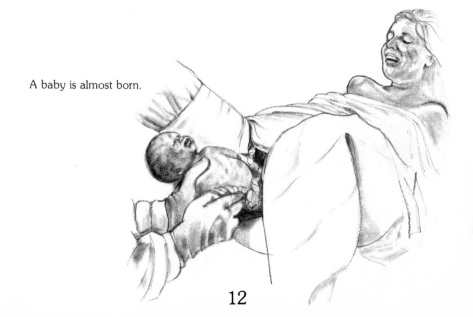

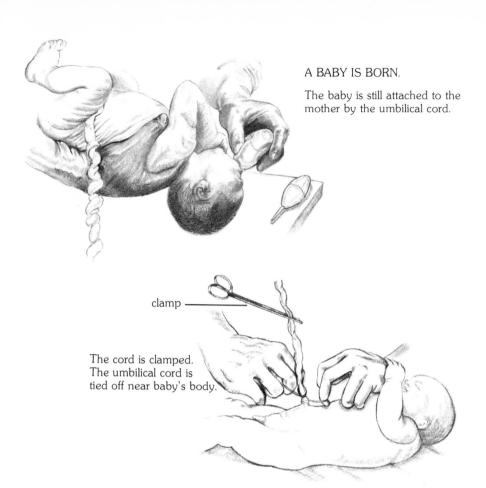

A BABY IS BORN.

The baby is still attached to the mother by the umbilical cord.

clamp

The cord is clamped.
The umbilical cord is
tied off near baby's body.

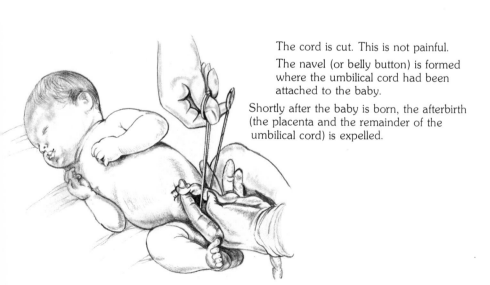

The cord is cut. This is not painful.

The navel (or belly button) is formed where the umbilical cord had been attached to the baby.

Shortly after the baby is born, the afterbirth (the placenta and the remainder of the umbilical cord) is expelled.

A woman knows she is ready to give birth when she feels muscle contractions in the uterus every 5-10 minutes. This is the signal that she will soon begin "labor"—the process of giving birth. It is called "labor" because the woman must work hard to push the baby down the birth canal so it can be born.

At birth the baby comes out, usually head first, through the vagina, which stretches as the baby is being born. Most children are born without physical handicaps, although sometimes injury to the brain or other parts of the body can occur during birth. Birth defects can also occur as a result of carelessness. Smoking, poor diet, alcohol, and some drugs can cause damage in the newborn. Prenatal (during pregnancy) care is very important for the health of the baby and for its mother. In addition, research has shown that a pregnant girl under eighteen faces higher risks medically. The younger the girl the greater the risk for both the mother and the new born child. The chances of a teenager giving birth to a premature or mentally retarded baby are much greater than if she gave birth in her early twenties.

The
Male

Most boys are developed sexually (reach puberty) between ages 12 and 15. Some reach puberty a little sooner, and some a little later. A boy will develop hair under his arms and around his genitals (sex organs).* The genitals are the penis ("dick," "prick," and "cock" are the street words for this organ) and the testicles ("balls" or "nuts" are the slang words.)

As a young man develops sexually, his penis becomes enlarged and erect (hard) once in a while, sometimes when he is thinking about sex and sometimes for no reason he can figure out. This happens to all males.

Boys often refer to their enlarged penis as an "erection," a "boner," or a "hard on." Whether erect or not, the size of the penis is not important. The size of the penis does not affect sexual pleasure.

---

*The hair around the sex organs is called "pubic hair" because the area around the sex organs is called the "pubis."

Along with its capacity to become enlarged and harder, the penis, when stimulated, will at times release semen—a whitish, sticky fluid which contains the sperm. (The sperm are produced in the testicles.) Both males and females can become sexually stimulated or excited by their thoughts, day or night dreams, by looking at "sexy" pictures, by touching or rubbing their genitals, by making love and in many other ways. The most intense pleasure from sexual stimulation (in males and females) is called an orgasm (climax).

To ejaculate (to release semen) is sometimes called "to come." When you are asleep and semen comes out, this is referred to as a nocturnal emission or a "wet dream." It is normal, and you should not worry about getting your underclothes or sheets messy. Parents know that this happens to all adolescent boys.

Male and female reproductive cells.

Sperm

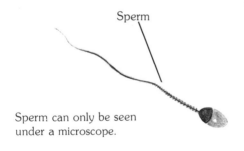

Sperm can only be seen under a microscope.

A single ejaculation contains millions of sperm.

Ovum (female egg)

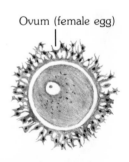

The female egg cell is the size of a grain of sand.

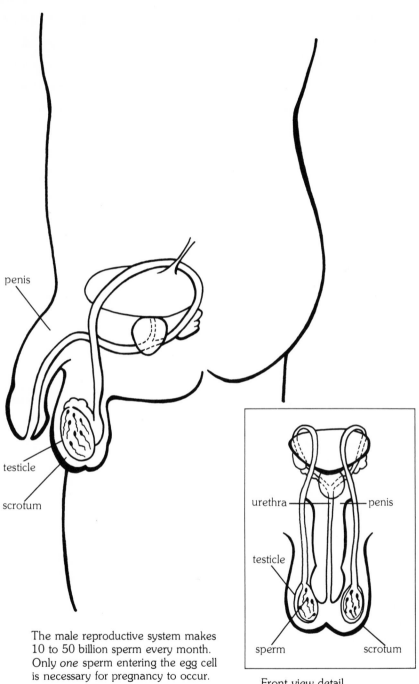

penis

testicle

scrotum

The male reproductive system makes
10 to 50 billion sperm every month.
Only *one* sperm entering the egg cell
is necessary for pregnancy to occur.

urethra — — penis

testicle

sperm   scrotum

Front view detail
of male reproductive organs.

Most boys enjoy rubbing or stimulating their penises because it is pleasurable and it helps reduce sexual tension. This is called masturbation, which sometimes results in an ejaculation. In language that is not polite, it is called "jerking off," "beating your meat," "whacking off," "jacking off" and a few other names.

Although some will deny it, almost all boys masturbate at one time or another. It is normal. As with all forms of sexual activity, masturbation should be done in private. Masturbation is not physically harmful even if done often. However, like everything else that is done "too much,"* it begins to lose its attraction and pleasure. If masturbation becomes "compulsive," which means a habit you can't control, then it is probably a sign of distress.

Many sexual thoughts and fantasies occur to boys when they masturbate. Just because you think of something, it doesn't mean you should or would do it. Sometimes in a fit of anger we think of wanting to hurt somebody; but that doesn't mean we are going to do it. At times we think of having sex with someone we know, even a close family member, but that doesn't mean we are seriously considering it.

*People usually ask, "How much is too much?" The answer is "once is too much if you don't enjoy it." Masturbation is a normal sexual expression for both males and females at any age.

18

When people marry, they may give up masturbation. Husbands and wives have sexual intercourse as a way of expressing love for each other, for pleasure, as well as for having children. This does not mean, however, that there is anything wrong with masturbation after marriage. When opportunities for sexual intercourse are not readily available, such as during a long period of absence or the later stages of pregnancy, masturbation is a normal way of satisfying sexual needs. Some people occasionally masturbate even when sexual intercourse is available because they enjoy the experience.

The
Female

Girls develop sexually earlier than boys—usually when they are about 10 or 11 years old, but some girls do not develop until they are 15 or 16 years old. Being developed sexually for a girl means she is able to become pregnant; her breasts increase in size, pubic hair grows around her vulva; and she begins to have her "period." The "period" (menstruation) lasts for a few days each month. This occurs in females who are not pregnant. When a woman is menstruating, blood-enriched tissue is discharged through the vagina. When a girl has her period, she wears a protective sanitary pad or tampon for her comfort and to prevent her clothing from being stained. Some women feel slightly ill or moody, or have cramps just before or during menstruation, but most engage in regular activities. A girl should shower or bathe daily during her period to prevent body odor. Some people refer to menstruation as their "friend," the "curse," being "on the rag," or being "unwell," but menstruation is not a sickness.

Many girls enjoy stimulating their genital areas because it is pleasurable and helps reduce sexual tension. This is called masturbation. Often a fluid is slowly discharged in the vagina. The clitoris is a source of sexual pleasure for the woman both in masturbation and during intercourse. Masturbation among females is normal, and is a problem only if it becomes "compulsive." If it is something you can't control, masturbation can increase sexual tension rather than reduce it. All sorts of thoughts and fantasies occur to girls when they are sexually stimulated.

The size and rate of growth of the breasts differs from girl to girl. A girl might notice that one breast is larger than the other—this often happens. Large or small, the size of a girl's breasts has nothing to do with her personal maturity or her sexuality.

What Is Love?

Young people often wonder if they are really "in love." You can love many people: your parents, friends, relatives, and others. Being "in love" usually refers to a powerful desire to be with and to please another person. When you are in love, you will want to have the respect and affection of the person you love. Although you may not always agree with that person's opinions, if you are in love, the two of you will settle your differences without trying to hurt each other. You will want him or her to be proud of you.

Some young people say they are in love, but at the same time neglect their studies or work, or become careless about their appearance and their actions when they are with the person they supposedly love. They try to attract attention by neglecting their health or taking foolish risks. Experience will show that this may be a "crush," sexual attraction, or immature attachment. It is also common among young people to "love" or hero-worship popular schoolmates and teachers as well as famous people whom they have never met. Real love is a shared intimacy, based on mutual respect and affection.

Sexual intercourse or sexual attraction is not the most important part of a loving relationship.

Of course, young people must also be able to accept disappointments. Sometimes you will fall in love with a person who does not return your love. If the other person doesn't show that he or she feels the same way after a reasonable time, you should look for someone else. Some adolescents think that being in love happens only once in a lifetime. This is not true. It is possible to be in love many times.

This may sound strange, but people who are involved in immature love affairs are often tired for no apparent reason. Those who are into the *real thing* are energized by the relationship. Check this out with your friends.

Sex
Before Marriage

Many young people have sexual relations before marriage (premarital sex). However, when sex is not related to love, it is often unsatisfying and can lead to emotional problems. One problem is the risk of unwanted pregnancy. Some girls have an abortion, which means ending a pregnancy in its early stages. Abortion, however, is an extremely dangerous operation *if not done by a doctor.**

Another problem with premarital sex is the risk of venereal disease (VD or as it is now commonly termed, STD—Sexually Transmitted Disease). Gonorrhea (sometimes called "clap") and syphilis are two very serious venereal diseases. VD is curable if discovered early and treated by a doctor. Unfortunately, the symptoms in women are not obvious; they don't always know they have it. A boy or girl can get VD the first time he or she has sexual contact with another person.

---

*Abortions early in pregnancy are simple and safe if done by a physician. If a teenager becomes pregnant, a medical abortion may be more moral than bringing an unwanted child into the world.

Sometimes a boy will say to a girl, "If you do not have sex with me, I won't take you out anymore." Any girl who has sex with such a boy is not very smart. He is not interested in the girl as a person, and in many cases the boy will not see the girl again after they have had sexual relations. Be on the alert for boys (and girls too) who use *lines* to get you to have sex. For example, "If you really loved me . . ." Why not respond by saying, "If you really loved me, you wouldn't put this kind of pressure on me."

There are many ways for adolescents and young adults to deal with their strong and healthy sexual urges without having sexual intercourse. Some of these are dating (which could involve kissing, necking and petting, often called "making out"*), masturbation, thinking and dreaming about sex, talking about it with a close friend, reading about it, discussing and kidding about sex in a group, or looking at magazines like *Playboy* and *Playgirl*. Young persons who are overly worried about sex and who neglect their work at school, their chores, etc., are probably feeling guilty about sex. Remember that all dreams, thoughts, and urges about sex are normal. Once you truly understand this, any *unpleasant* sexual thoughts and urges you have will last only a short while, and will not be very upsetting. (Of course, you may want to fully enjoy the *pleasurable* sexual thoughts and feelings that you get.)

*Intense physical contact with a person you don't really care about, however, is often not a pleasant experience. It could lead to an increase of tension rather than provide an outlet for sexual urges.

Some people boast a lot about sex. In most cases, they are either not telling the truth or they suffer from feelings of inferiority. Sometimes groups of boys or girls discuss sex among themselves. This will not be an embarrassing situation for those who know the facts.

Sex Problems

There are youth and adults who have serious sex problems. Some may want to have sexual relations with children. There are men who are so disturbed that they force others to have sex with them. This is called rape. A woman who has intercourse with men for money is called a prostitute or whore (pronounced hore).

Some men may find that they are impotent (unable to have an erection when they want to have intercourse), or they may ejaculate prematurely ("come" before or immediately upon putting the penis into the vagina). Some women don't enjoy sex, or even if they do, they don't have an orgasm (sometimes this is called frigidity). For both men and women, this may be a temporary situation.

It could be due to guilt, inexperience, or unfavorable conditions often associated with first experiences with sex. Occasionally, it may be due to a physical problem. It can also be the result of the partner not being sensitive enough about her (or his) sexual and emotional needs. Sexual difficulties of this kind are usually solved when two people work at their problems with love and understanding for each other. If problems persist, professional help should be found.

Some people are "always on the make," which means that they often talk about and want to have sex with someone, but they are not really interested in that someone as a person. Young people "on the make," whether they know it or not, fear and dislike the opposite sex. Because they are unsure about their own sexuality they think they can "prove" something by having many sexual experiences. The fact is that no matter how often they have sex, they are rarely satisfied, even though they may boast about their experiences.

In any case, sexual intercourse by itself is never a test or a proof of love. It can be and often is an aspect of a loving relationship. It can also be an expression of violence (as in rape) or hostility (as when it is used to exploit another person).

Sex Differences

Many young people would like to remain virgins until marriage and some remain celibate (do not have sexual intercourse) their entire life. Both of these options are normal. These days people are considering such choices as remaining single (without excluding sex) and marrying, but without having children.

Some people prefer to have sexual experiences with persons of their own sex. They are called homosexuals.* Most boys and girls have homosexual thoughts occasionally. Some even have homosexual experiences. This doesn't mean that they are homosexual. The people properly called homosexuals are those who, as adults, prefer to have sexual contacts *only* with persons of their own sex.

Homosexual behavior is illegal in some states of the union, but most religious and professional groups are opposed to laws which interfere with the private sexual behavior between consenting adults. Some people enjoy sexual relations with both sexes throughout their adult life. They are called bisexuals. Modern psychologists no longer see homosexual or bisexual behavior between consenting adults as a problem or disorder.

*The popular words for male homosexuals is "gay" and for females, "lesbians". Some negative expressions for gay men are "faggot," "fruit," and "queer;" and for females, "dyke."

Prevention of Pregnancy

There are several ways in which women can prevent pregnancy when they have sexual intercourse. One way is to take birth control pills which are prescribed by a doctor. They must be taken regularly. Some people think that if you take the "pill" once or twice it is enough. This is not true. The "pill" is one type of contraceptive,* and is widely used for birth control and family planning. Pills are not suitable for everyone, and that is why they should be taken only under medical supervision. Another method of birth control is a device known as a diaphragm. A woman must be fitted for a diaphragm by a doctor, who will show her how to place it in the vagina. The diaphragm prevents the sperm from reaching the ovum (egg cell). A diaphragm must be used with a contraceptive jelly or cream, or it will not be effective. Another birth control method is the IUD (Intrauterine Device). It is inserted by a doctor and remains in the uterus until the doctor is asked to remove it. Contraceptive foams for women (inserted into the vagina before sexual intercourse) are available in drugstores without a prescription.

Douching and feminine hygiene products are *not* birth controls.

*A contraceptive is a device used for the purpose of preventing pregnancy. While contraceptives "work" most of the time, they are not 100 percent effective.

A man can also use a contraceptive. It is called a condom (rubber) which is available without a prescription at a drugstore (and in some states from a vending machine). It is sometimes called a "safety" or a "Trojan." A condom is a contraceptive that also helps prevent VD. The rubber is rolled onto the erect penis just before intercourse; thus, the sperm goes into the rubber instead of the vagina. When the man pulls his penis out of the vagina he should hold onto the rubber so that it does not slip off. Rubbers should be used only once. The male use of the condom combined with the female use of contraceptive foam is a good form of birth control, especially when medical methods are not available. Another approach is for the man to pull his penis out of the vagina (withdrawal) before he comes. This is generally not "safe" and it is not sexually satisfying, but it is certainly better than no method at all.

Questions About Sex

Of the thousands of questions about sex that high school students asked me, the following ten were the most common.

1. Do you think it's right to have sexual intercourse at our ages . . . 15, 16, 17 . . .?

I have already suggested that it is not a good idea, and I am sure this answer will not satisfy some readers. I think it's wrong for teenagers to risk pregnancy, venereal disease, or to make immature decisions such as confusing crushes and infatuations with love. In addition, sexual intercourse with a person you don't love or respect is seldom satisfying and can result in sexual problems. Older working or college youth who love each other and can easily arrange for contraceptives and privacy may want to make their own decisions about premarital sex. We hope that their decisions will be based on mutual respect.

Some young people feel that they have already made mistakes because of sex experiments. They need worry *only* if they have not profited from their experiences. We all make mistakes sometimes. Of course, we have to be especially careful when other people can be hurt. At the same time, we should not exaggerate the meaning of all sexual "mistakes." It is possible during adolescence to have sexual experiences with the opposite or the same sex without any undesirable effects. My point, though, is that the risk of unhappy or even tragic consequences is great. It is also sad to note that most boys—as many as 85%—will eventually abandon the teenage girls they make pregnant and even the girls they marry.

2. Does "jerking off" frequently cause any harmful effects later?

"Jerking off" (masturbation), no matter how frequently it is done, does not cause any physical harm. The shame or guilt that some people feel about it is what can be harmful. It is absolutely *not true,* as some people claim, that masturbation can cause insanity, acne or blindness, or that boys can use up sperm that is essential for reproduction later on. The male testes produce all the sperm needed, no matter how frequently a person masturbates.

3. Can a girl become pregnant when she has intercourse for the first time?

Yes. There is no absolutely "safe" time for having sexual intercourse without risking pregnancy. The risk is greatly reduced with contraception. In addition, a woman whose periods are regular is less likely to become pregnant during her menstrual period or two or three days before or after it.

4. Is there a way of telling what is normal or abnormal sex between two people?

This is a difficult question, but I will give you my opinion. If we assume the people involved are ready for sexual experiences, sexual "acts" can be considered "normal" ("mature" might be a better word) if the following conditions exist:

The behavior is voluntary. A person chooses to do it and it isn't something a person does because he can't help it.

The behavior is enjoyable and both partners consent to it.

The behavior is not exploitive. It is free of guilt and serves to enrich the relationship.

5. How can you tell if you have VD (venereal disease)?

Venereal disease results from having sexual or close physical relations with a person (homosexual or heterosexual) who is infected. An individual most likely to spread VD is one who is promiscuous (a person who has sexual relations with many people). Three common venereal diseases are gonorrhea, syphilis, and genital herpes.

The first sign of gonorrhea for men and women often is a burning sensation in the sex organ when urinating. This would be noticed about two to six or more days after sexual relations with an infected person. Pus often drips from the penis. One of the big problems is that many women (and some men) do not have obvious symptoms and are unaware that they have gonorrhea.

The first sign of syphilis is a single sore (usually around the genitals), followed by a rash on any part of the body, appearing from ten days to as much as three months after contact. While these signs may disappear, they will soon be replaced by fever, headache and sore throat. Untreated gonorrhea and syphilis infections, despite eventual disappearance of outside signs, remain active in the body and can be the cause of sterility, blindness, insanity, and other crippling conditions. Syphilis can also result in death. Most venereal diseases, when discovered early and treated by a doctor, can be cured.

Herpes causes painful blisters on the genitals or anus. Except for pregnant women, it is not as serious as gonorrhea or syphilis, but causes much discomfort.

Male use of the condom (rubber) and both partners urinating and washing with soap and warm water immediately after intercourse will reduce the risk of VD. With more than three million new cases each year, VD has become the most serious communicable (catching) disease in this country. All states permit clinics, Planned Parenthood Centers and private physicians to test for and treat VD without parental knowledge or consent. Doctors should be told what types of sexual activity were involved so that proper tests can be made.

6. How long is the average-size penis?

The average size of an erect penis (a "hard on") is between five and six inches. In actual practice it does not matter whether the penis is more or less than "average." The notion that size is important for satisfactory sexual relations is not true. Some males make judgments about size by comparing their nonerect penis with others they may see at home or in a public shower or bathroom. There is no relationship between the way a penis appears when it is soft and when it is hard (erect).

7. Why does a boy's penis sometimes get hard when he is with a girl?

A boy's penis becomes hard when it is stimulated—often due to physical closeness to another person, or sexual thoughts, but sometimes for reasons that are not completely understood. Many boys find their penis erect upon awakening in the morning or when exposed to cold. Some boys have frequent erections. This is perfectly normal. As boys get older they find they have more control over their erections.

8. What causes homosexuality?

Most professionals no longer believe that homosexuality is a disease or a disorder. It is estimated that there are about 20 million homosexuals in the United States. Homosexuals exist in every culture and society. In any case, we now know that homosexual experiences are not rare during childhood and adolescence. These experiences do not necessarily mean that a person will become an adult homosexual. Many young people who have had more than just a few homosexual experiences have been known to marry successfully. It is completely untrue that if you have homosexual thoughts or dreams you must be a homosexual. Mature people are aware of the fact that they have both homosexual and heterosexual feelings, even though the majority of them prefer sexual activities with members of the opposite sex. In this connection, you should know that one cannot judge by appearance whether a person is a homosexual. Some feminine-looking men and masculine-looking women are heterosexual, and some highly "masculine," so-called muscular all-American types or feminine-looking women are homosexual. We do not know why people are or become homosexuals.

9. Is it abnormal to use the mouth in sex play?

No. Some couples put their mouths on each other's genitals and for them it is a pleasurable preliminary to, or substitute for, sexual intercourse.

10. How come most parents don't tell their children about sex?

Some parents think that knowledge is harmful: "If you tell children about sex, they'll do it."

Some parents think that sex is dirty.

Some parents wait too long before they talk about it, and when they do, their children are unwilling or are too embarrassed to listen. Many parents simply do not know what to say or how much to say about sex.

If parents are askable, children ask questions at three, four and five years of age. It's about time parents realized that they are the main sex educators of their children, whether they do it well or badly. They might as well do a good job of it and begin by telling the truth!

Conclusion

A lot of young people ask me if orgasm is the main thing in sex. Usually girls are the only ones who are supposed to have trouble reaching orgasm (climax). It is not generally known, but the fact is that boys do not always have an orgasm during ejaculation. Often they do, but not always—and the orgasm varies in strength and pleasure. Both men and women are able to enjoy sex without orgasm. It is rare for a couple to have orgasms at the same time during their first experiences. Some couples never have mutual orgasms. Couples who have healthy sexual attitudes and who are not overly concerned about their orgasms enjoy sex the most. Besides we need to get away from seeing sex as a kind of gymnastics. If I were to think of the ten most important aspects of a marital relationship, love, caring and intimacy would be number one; two, a sense of humor; three, honest communication; nine, sexual fulfillment; ten, sharing household tasks. What, in your opinion, would be numbers 4, 5, 6, 7, and 8?

I hope this book has been helpful. If you want to know more about sex, the following list of books and pamphlets will guide you. If, for some reason, you are still worried about sex and your parents have not been able to help you, ask your parents to arrange a meeting with a psychologist or a doctor who specializes in adolescent problems. If you feel you cannot talk to your parents at first, try talking to a sympathetic school counselor or teacher. You can also contact Planned Parenthood or a "hot line" in your community. Once you know and understand sex, it becomes just one part of life.

Remember, too, that being masculine for boys and feminine for girls means a great deal more than sexual intercourse. Most of all it means feeling secure. It means accepting yourself for what you are and having faith in what you can become. It means no one can make you feel inferior without your consent.

Selected References
Books Distributed by Ed-U Press

For Teenagers and Young Adults

The New You by Sol Gordon. The author describes this book as his most personal, most spiritual and most important work. Consists of poems, essays, slogans. 1979. $1.95.

YOU — A Survival Guide for Youth by Sol Gordon. Designed to communicate essential life knowledge and enhance self-acceptance among youth. $6.95.

You Would If You Loved Me by Sol Gordon. Sex lines heard and used by youth. Includes responses. 1979. $1.25.

Facts About VD For Today's Youth by Sol Gordon. Describes VD, how to recognize symptoms, how and where to get medical treatment, and how to prevent VD. Written in clear and simple language. 1979. $3.50.

Ten Heavy Facts About Sex. Comic book. What kids want to know. $.45.

VD Claptrap. Comic book. Straight info about syphilis and gonorrhea, including methods of prevention. $.45.

Protect Yourself From Becoming An Unwanted Parent. Comic book. Concise info on birth control methods. Cost: same as above.

Juice Use — Special hangover Edition. Comic book. A non-conventional approach on alcohol. Includes a lover's alert, and sections on sex hang-ups and boredom. Cost: same as above.

For Younger Children

Girls Are Girls And Boys Are Boys — So What's The Difference? Completely revised edition of Sol Gordon's non-sexist, liberating sex education book for children aged 6-10. Stunning illustrations by Vivien Cohen. $3.95.

Did The Sun Shine Before You Were Born? — A Sex Education Primer by Sol and Judith Gordon. Paperback for children aged 3-7. Developed to help parents communicate facts about sex, reproduction and the family to their children. $3.50.

For Professionals, Group Leaders, University Courses, And Parents

The Sexual Adolescent by Sol Gordon, Peter Scales, and Kathleen Everly. 1979. Extensive review of sex education research and programs, suggestions for creative action, annotated bibliography, and much more. $8.95.

Community Sex Education Programs For Parents: A Training Manual For Organizers. A comprehensive approach to community programming. 116pp. $4.00.

Sexuality Today and Tomorrow Contemporary Issues in Human Sexuality. Sol Gordon and Roger Libby (Eds.) Social, political and personal issues concerning sexuality and sex roles and their inter-relationship in contemporary society. $8.95.

Sex Education: The Parent's Role by Sol Gordon and Irving R. Dickman. Public Affairs Pamphlet No. 549. Valuable information in a concise, handy format. $.50.

Parenting — A Guide For Young People by Sol Gordon and Mina Wollin. A thoroughly modern exposition to prepare potential parents for mature parenting roles. Geared to senior high school and community college levels. $3.95.

Psychology For You by Sol Gordon. A 500pp. humanistic text for senior high schools and community colleges. 1978. $7.95.

Techniques For Leading Group Discussions On Human Sexuality by Winifred Kempton. $1.00

Audio-Visuals

How To Teach Your Child About Sex. Cassette. Sex educator Gordon discusses what, when, and how to tell children about sex. He explains how to answer questions, and shows how attitudes have changed since the inception of the women's movement. Produced by Cassette Communications, Inc. N.Y. $8.95.

Coming to Terms With Your Own Sexuality First. Cassette. Knowledge about sex is not harmful and you don't have to be comfortable to sex educate your child are two of the many important sex education concepts conveyed by Sol Gordon in this 60-minute humorous presentation. $7.95

The Politics Of Sexuality. 1979. Cassette. With an emphasis on preparing today's youth for tomorrow's families, Sol Gordon discusses relationships between the sexes, values, how to recognize a mature relationship, discovering and responding to lines and other important concepts in curriculum development. $7.95.

How Can You Tell If You Are Really In Love? 1979. Sol Gordon defines mature and immature love, discusses the elements of successful relationships, and urges clarification of values to avoid damaging involvements. Cassette $8.50. Full color filmstrip, cassette, guide $17.50.

Kids Who Have Kids Are Kidding Themselves by Sol Gordon. 1979. Startling statistics and truths about teenage pregnancies will help youth realistically understand this event. Includes "You Would If You Loved Me." Full color filmstrip, cassette, guide, book. $18.50.

Getting It Together Is Life Itself by Sol Gordon. Exciting new production of this proven classroom tool that focuses on students' real problems and presents some possible solutions. Provokes electric, thoughtful "raps" that help students "get themselves together." Full color filmstrip, cassette, guide. $17.50.

This Is You. Complete program of *Kids Who Have Kids Are Kidding Themselves, How Can You Tell If You Are Really In Love, And Getting It Together Is Life Itself.* 3 filmstrips, 3 cassettes, 3 guides, book. See description above. $51.00.

Herpie — The New VD Around Town! Filmstrip, audio cassette and study guide. An innovative approach to teach young people about this dangerous venereal disease by The Creative Media Group. Filmstrip/cassette $35.

Breaking The Language Barrier. Desensitizes the language of sex as it matches slang terms with their conventional and clinical counterparts. Filmstrip $25.

Teenage Parents Always Have Homework. 1979. Poster. Baby in high chair dramatically portrays this difficult life situation for youth. Developed by the Inter-Agency Council on Mental Retardation and Creative Media Group. $2.00.

About The Handicapped

Love, Sex And Birth Control For The Mentally Retarded — A Guide For Parents. $1.00.

Amor, Sexo, Y Control De La Natalidad Para El Retardado Mental. Spanish edition of Love, Sex and Birth Control for the Mentally Retarded. $1.00.

Living Fully: A Guide For Young People With A Handicap, Their Parents, Their Teachers, And Professionals by Sol Gordon, Charles Weening, Betty Lou Kratoville, Doug Biklen. $8.95.

Sexual Rights For The People . . . Who Happen To Be Handicapped. 1979. A ten-page article that deals with practical information. Includes a selected reading list. $1.00.

Feeling Good About Yourself: A Resource Guide and Curriculum for Social Esteem, and Human Sexuality Available from Academic Therapy Publications, 20 Commercial Blvd., Novato, CA 94947.

Resources From Other Sources

Paperback Books for Teenagers Who Want to Know More

The Teenage Body Book by Kathy McCoy and Charles Wibbelsman. Wallaby/Pocket Books.

Sex, With Love: A Guide for Young People by Eleanor Hamilton. Beacon Press.

Learning About Sex: The Contemporary Guide for Young Adults by Gary F. Kelly. Barron's Educational Series, Inc.

The Heart of Loving by Eugene Kennedy. Argus Communications.

Notes on Love and Courage by Hugh Prather. Doubleday and Co.

Love by Leo Buscaglia. Fawcet Books.

Changes: You and Your Body. A wonderful booklet prepared by CHOICE, 1501 Cherry St., Philadelphia, PA 19102.

Discovering Yourself I and *Discovering Yourself II.* Two excellent anthologies of articles that have appeared in *Teen* magazine written mainly by Kathy McCoy. Available from *Teen* magazine, Peterson Publishing Co., 6725 Sunset Blvd., Los Angeles, CA 90028.

Boys and Sex and *Girls And Sex.* Both by Wardell B. Pomeroy, Dell Publishing Co., Inc.

Best Films and Filmstrips

Perennial Education, Inc., 477 Roger Williams, PO Box 885, Ravinia, Highland Park, IL 60035.

Parenthood: A Series. Filmstrip and cassette tapes covering preparation for parenthood, pregnancy, preparation for birth, and birth. From Guidance Associates, Box 300, White Plains, NY 10602.

For VD Information, Call:

National Operation Venus: 800-523-1885 (toll free)

For Additional Information, Write:

American Medical Association, Department of Community Health and Health Education, 535 North Dearborn St., Chicago, IL 60610

American School Health Association, 107 South Depeyster St., Kent, OH 44240

Institute for Family Research and Education, 760 Ostrom Ave., Syracuse, NY 13210

National Alliance for Optional Parenthood, 2010 Massachusetts Ave., N.W., Washington, D.C. 20036

National Council of Churches, Commission on Marriage and the Family, 475 Riverside Dr., New York, NY 10027

The National Foundation/March of Dimes, Box 2000, White Plains, NY 10602

The National PTA, 700 North Rush St., Chicago, IL 60611

Planned Parenthood-World Population, 810 Seventh Ave., New York, NY 10019

Population Institute, 100 Maryland Ave., Washington, D.C. 20002

Population Reference Bureau, 1337 Connecticut Ave., N.W., Washington, D.C. 20036

Public Affairs Pamphlets, 381 Park Avenue So., New York, NY 10010

Sex Information and Education Council of the U.S. (SIECUS), 84 Fifth Ave., Room 407, New York, NY 10001

Synagogue Council of America, Committee on the Family, 432 Park Avenue So., New York, NY 10016

United States Catholic Conference, Family Life Bureau, 1312 Massachusetts Ave., N.W., New York, NY 10016

Zero Population Growth, 1346 Connecticut Ave., N.W., Washington, D.C. 20036

If You're Facing A Problem of Censorship, Contact:

The Student Press Law Center, 1033 30th St., N.W., Washington, D.C. 20007,or your local chapter of the American Civil Liberties Union.

Some Thoughts And Definitions Of Love

"Love is not boastful, or conceited, or rude; love is patient, kind, and without envy."

I Corinthians

X 111, 14

"When the satisfaction or security of another person becomes as significant to one as is one's own satisfaction or security, then the state of love exists."

Harry Stack Sullivan, Psychiatrist

"The most unsatisfactory men are those who pride themselves on their virility and regard sex as if it were some sort of athletics at which you win cups. It is a woman's spirit and mood a man has to stimulate in order to make sex interesting. The real lover is the man who can thrill you by just touching your hand and smiling into your eyes."

Marilyn Monroe, *My Story*

"The tragic mistake is to assume that any treasure, person, or object, must be possessed to be loved."

Ethel Sabin Smith

"Love is the overwhelming desire and persistent effort of one person to create for another person the condition which that other person can become the man or woman God meant them to be."

William H. Genne, Theologian

"The only abnormality is the incapacity to love."

Anais Nin

"It has been wisely said that we cannot really love anybody at whom we never laugh."

Agnes Repplier. *Reader's Digest,* Aug. 1962

"The truth is that there is only one terminal dignity — Love. And the story of a love is not important. What is important is that one is capable of love. It is perhaps the only glimpse we are permitted of eternity."

Helen Hayes. *Guideposts,* Jan., 1960.

NATIONAL FAMILY SEX EDUCATION WEEK

October 4-10, 1981

PREPARE TODAY'S YOUTH
FOR
TOMORROW'S FAMILY

For more information on this October Event, Write

The Institute for Family Research and Education
760 Ostrom Ave.

Syracuse, New York 13210